The Father Ch
Joke Book fc

Compiled by Hugh Morrison

Montpelier Publishing
London 2014

ISBN-13: 978-1505420906

Published by Montpelier Publishing, London.

Printed by Amazon Createspace.

Christmas jokes

What sweets does Father Christmas eat?
Polar mints!

What fruit does the Queen eat on Christmas Day?
The Queen's peach!

What's small, lies in a crib and goes in sandwiches?
The baby cheeses!

Little Johnny woke up on Christmas morning and rushed to his stocking to see what Father Christmas had brought him. The stocking was empty, except for a note which said 'Presents not delivered. Child awake at time of delivery.'

What kind of Christmas play do insects perform?
A gnativity play!

Man: What would it take for you to kiss me under the mistletoe?
Woman: Anaesthetic.

What's the worst Christmas present you can get?
A set of batteries with a label saying 'toys not included.'

Little Johnny: Mum, can I have a cat for Christmas?
Mum: No, you'll have turkey like the rest of us!

Twelve things to say about presents you don't like
1. How lovely! Just like the one in the charity shop window!
2. I hope the dustman doesn't take it away by accident.
3. It'll be perfect for wearing at home. With the curtains drawn.
4. If the dog buries it, I'll be very angry.
5. I think you've got my present mixed up with the stuff for the jumble sale.
6. I'll share it with my brother. In fact, I'll *give* it to him.
7. Isn't this what I gave *you* last year?
8. Where's the receipt?
9. I think I prefer the wrapping paper.
10. To save you embarrassment I'll give you my views in the thank you letter.
11. It's better to give than receive. You can have it back.
12. Can Grandad wear it until I grow into it?

What's it called when you do sums on Christmas Eve?
Midnight maths!

Christmas tip: never try to catch snowflakes with your tongue until the birds have flown south for winter.

A Christmas card greeting:
Don't worry about the past, it's over and done with.
Don't worry about the future, it hasn't happened yet.
Don't worry about the present – I didn't get you one either!

What Christmas carol is a favourite with parents?
Silent Night.

A girl and her mother were putting out mince pies by the fireplace for Father Christmas to eat when he arrived. The mother accidentally dropped one of the pies on the floor. She picked it up, dusted it and put it back on the plate. 'Father Christmas will never know,' she said to her daughter. The little girl looked puzzled. 'So he knows if I've been bad or good, but he doesn't know his mince pie fell on the floor?'

'I wish it could be Christmas every day' goes the song. But then when would we do our Christmas shopping?!

How does a snowman lose weight?
He just waits for spring!

What do ghosts watch at Christmas time?
A phantomime!

What says 'ho ho ho' and smells?
Farter Christmas!

What do vegetarians want for Christmas?
Peas on earth!

How can angels fly?
Because they take themselves lightly!

On Christmas Eve a policeman found a man on the pavement who
had been run over.

'Did you get the registration number?' the policeman asked.
'No,' said the man, 'but I'd recognise those reindeer anywhere.'

Mum: What are you writing to Father Christmas, Johnny?

Little Johnny: Well I lost my present list, so I'm telling him just to send me all the stuff he forgot to send last year.

What do you say to a stressed snowman?
Chill out!

Why is December a hot month?
Because it has an 'ember' in it!

What does a snowman put on his face at night?
Cold cream!

On Christmas eve, a vicar was giving his sermon in church. All of a sudden, there was a power cut and all the lights went out. When the lights came back on a few minutes later, the vicar looked through his notes and asked, 'where was I?' Somebody shouted out 'right near the end!'

What do you get if you cross Father Christmas with a detective?
Santa Clues!

How does Father Christmas kill people?
He sleighs them!

What do you get if you cross Santa and a dog?
Santa Paws!

What did one snowman say to the other snowman?
Ice to meet you!

What kind of mobile phone does Father Christmas use?
Pay as you ho, ho, ho!

What do you call a Christmas duck?
A Christmas quacker!

Why is Father Christmas good at karate?
Because he has a black belt!

What do you use to drain the Brussels sprouts with?
An Advent colander!

What do you make if you mix flour with snow?
Frosty the Doughman!

What is a snowman's favourite drink?
Ice tea!

Little Johnny was opening his Christmas presents. 'Did you like them, dear?' asked his mother.

'Yes,' replied Johnny. 'But they all say "From Father Christmas". When do I get the ones from you and daddy?'

Where do snowmen go to dance?
A snow ball!

When does Christmas come before Halloween?
In the dictionary!

Why did Father Christmas become ill when he came down the chimney?
Because he caught the flue!

Where do they make films about Christmas?
Holly-wood!

Why did the snowman call his dog 'Frost'?
Because frost bites!

What do angry mice send each other at Christmas?
Cross mouse cards!

A father was buying a train set on Christmas Eve. 'This is a lovely train set, sir,' said the shop assistant. 'I'm sure you'll son will love it.' 'In that case,' said the father, 'I'll take two sets!'

What comes at the end of Christmas?
The letter 's'!

What do snowmen ride on?
Icicles!

What's Father Christmas' favourite 1970s pop band?
Sleighed! (Slade)

What kind of singers are useful when you've bought Christmas presents?
Rappers!

What's red and white and black all over?
Father Christmas after he comes down the chimney!

What's a snowman's favourite Chinese food?
Stir fried ice with chilly sauce!

An old lady had no money for food so she wrote a letter to Father Christmas. It said 'Dear Father Christmas, I've got nobody left to look after me. So please send me £100 for Christmas so I can buy some food.' She addressed the envelope to Father Christmas, North Pole, Greenland.

The postmen in the post office didn't really believe in Father Christmas. But they felt very sorry for the old lady so they passed round a hat and managed to collect £90. They sent the money back to the old lady signed 'From Father Christmas.'

When the old lady received the money she wrote a thank you letter to Father Christmas. 'Dear Father Christmas,' it went, 'thank you for the £90. But I did ask for £100, so £10 was missing. I think those rotten postmen must have stolen it!'

What do Christmas stockings sing?
Silent night, holey night!

What does a cat get on the beach at Christmas?
Sandy claws!

What do sheep say at Christmas?
Season's bleatings!

Teacher: What are you giving your parents for Christmas, Johnny?
Little Johnny: A list of everything I want!

What do you get if you cross Father Christmas with a duck?
A Christmas quacker!

What did Father Christmas' wife say when she looked at the sky?
'Looks like rain, dear.'

What part of the body only appears at Christmas?
The mistle-toe!

What falls down when it's born, lies still when it's alive, and runs when it's dead?
Snow.

What did the monkey sing at Christmas?
Jungle bells!

What's the best key to get at Christmas?
A tur-key!

What kind of camera does Father Christmas use?
A North Pole-aroid!

Twelve ways to confuse Father Christmas

1. Instead of mince pies, leave him a salad, and a note explaining that he needs to lose weight.
2. While he's in the house, find his sleigh and write him a parking ticket.
3. Keep an angry bull in your living room. If you think a bull goes crazy when he sees a little red cape, wait until he sees that fat man in a red suit!
4. Build an army of mean-looking snowmen on the roof, holding signs that say 'We hate Christmas,' and 'Go away Father Christmas.'
5. Leave a note by the telephone, telling Father Christmas his wife called and wanted to remind him to pick up some milk and a loaf of bread on his way home.
6. Leave a plate filled with mince pies and a glass of milk out, with a note that says, 'For The Tooth Fairy.'
7. Take everything out of your house as if it's just been robbed. When Father Christmas arrives, appear dressed like a policeman and say, 'Well, well. They always return to the scene of the crime.'
8. Leave out a copy of your Christmas list with last-minute changes and corrections.
9. Set a bear trap at the bottom of the chimney. Wait for Father Christmas to get caught in it, and then explain that you're sorry, but from a distance, he looked like a bear.
10. Leave out a Father Christmas suit, with an attached dry-cleaning bill.

11. Paint hoof-prints all over your face and clothes. While he's in the house, go out on the roof. When he comes back up, act like you've been trampled. Threaten to sue for personal injury.
12. Instead of ornaments, decorate your tree with Easter eggs.

Which of Father Christmas' reindeer has bad manners?
Rude-olph!

What's the difference between the Christmas alphabet and the ordinary alphabet?
The Christmas alphabet has NOEL!

What do fishes sing at Christmas?
Christmas corals!

Why are Christmas trees such bad knitters?
They are always dropping their needles.

Where does a snowman keep his money?
In a snow bank.

What does Santa Claus feel when he gets stuck up a chimney?
Claus-trophobic!

Teacher (to pupil): I told everyone to bring in something to do with Christmas and put it on your desks. Why have you brought that bucket of water?
Pupil: It's last year's snowman, sir!

It was Christmas in the court room and a prisoner was brought in.
The judge asked the policeman why he had been arrested.
'For doing his Christmas shopping early,' said the policeman.
'That's no crime,' said the judge.
'It is if you do it before the shops are open,' said the officer.

Why couldn't Mary and Joseph play cards?
They only had three kings!

What's the best kind of Christmas king?
A stoc-king!

Why did nobody like the icicle when the sun came out?
Because he was such a drip!

What do you get when you cross a snowman with a vampire?
Frostbite.

The four stages of life:
1. You believe in Father Christmas.
2. You don't believe in Father Christmas.
3. You dress up as Father Christmas
4. You look like Father Christmas!

What's the most popular Christmas carol in the desert?
Camel ye faithful!

What do snowmen eat for breakfast?
Frosted Flakes!

What nationality is Father Christmas?

North Polish!

What's green, sits by the Christmas tree and goes 'ribbit!'
Mistle-toad!

How do you know when there's a snowman in your bed?
You wake up wet!

What do snowmen sing at a birthday party?
Freeze a jolly good fellow!

How much did Father Christmas pay for his sleigh?
Nothing, it was on the house!

Two snowmen were in a field. One turned to the other and said 'I don't know about you but I can smell carrots!'

What do you say to a blind reindeer?
I have no eye deer!

Did you hear about the man who stole an Advent calendar?
He got 25 days!

Where does Father Christmas stay on holiday?
At a ho-ho-hotel!

What kind of motorbike does Father Christmas ride?
A Holly Davidson!

What do you call a snowman in the summer?
A puddle!

What's black and white and red all over?
Santa covered with chimney soot.

What disease do Christmas decorations get?
Tinsilitis!

What do you get if you cross an apple and a Christmas tree?
A pineapple!

Why did the turkey join the band?
Because it had two drumsticks!

A contestant on a TV quiz programme was asked to name two of Father Christmas' reindeer. The contestant said, 'Rudolph and Olive!'

The host said, 'We'll accept Rudolph but there's no reindeer called Olive.'

'Of course there is,' said the man. 'You know, "Olive the other reindeer, used to laugh and call him names..."'

What never eats at Christmas time?
The turkey - it's always stuffed!

What do snowmen wear on their heads?
Ice caps!

What part of a reindeer smells the most?
His nose!

What does a Christmas tree wear on its head?
A bauble hat!

What's the favourite wine at Christmas?
'I don't like Brussels sprouts!'

What do you have in December that you don't have in any other month?
The letter D!

What does Father Christmas eat for breakfast?
Mistle-toast!

What goes 'oh, oh, oh'?
Father Christmas talking backwards!

What does a cat on the beach have in common with Christmas?
Sandy claws!

What's brown and creeps round the kitchen?
A mince spy!

Where do you find reindeer?
It depends on where you leave them!

How does a Christmas tree die?
It just pines away!

What do you get from a drunken cow?
Brandy butter!

What's red and white, red and white, red and white?
Father Christmas rolling down a hill!

What did the stamp say to the Christmas card?
'Stick with me and we'll go places!'

What's fat and visits Bethlehem?
The Three Wide Men!

What kind of owl do you get in a nativity play?
The Angel Gabri-owl!

How does Good King Wenceslas like his pizza?
Deep pan, crisp and even!

What's the best thing to put in a Christmas pudding?
Your teeth!

What has wings but cannot fly?
Roast turkey!

What did Adam say the day before Christmas?
It's Christmas, Eve!

Why does Father Christmas always come down the chimney?
Because it 'soots' him!

Why should you go to Istanbul for Christmas?
Because you're surrounded by Turkey!

Why do reindeers have fur coats?
Because they'd look silly in plastic macs!

Did you have grandma for Christmas dinner?
No, we had turkey!

Christmas books

Around the World in Eighty Sleighs
By Ray N. Deer

Earlier Every Year
By Chris Mass

You Gave us Something Last Year
By Carol Singer

My First Performance
By Nat Ivvity

The Big Bang
By Paul A. Cracker

Nobody Loves Me
By Russel Sprouts

Won't Somebody Kiss Me?
By Miss L. Toe

No Room at the Inn
By Beth Lee Hemm

Christmas knock knock jokes

Knock knock!
Who's there?
Snow!
Snow who?
Snow use, I've forgotten my name!

Knock knock!
Who's there?
Frank!
Frank who?
Frankincense!

Knock knock!
Who's there?
Miss!
Miss who?
Miss L. Toe!

Knock-Knock.
Who's there?
Tree!
Tree who?
Tree wise men!

Knock, knock
Who's there?
Mary and Abbey
Mary and Abbey who?
Mary Christmas and Abbey New Year!

Knock knock!
Who's there?
Carol!
Carol who?
Carol Singer!

Knock Knock!
Who's there?
Anna!
Anna who?
Anna Partridge in a Pear Tree!

Funny carols

We four lads of Liverpool are
John in a taxi
George in a car
Paul on his scooter
Tooting the hooter
Following Ringo Starr!

While shepherds washed their socks by night
All seated round the tub,
A bar of Sunlight soap came down,
And they began to scrub!

We three kings in Leicester Square
Selling ladies' underwear
No elastic
How fantastic
Very unsafe to wear!

Good King Wenceslas looked out
Of his bedroom window.
Silly sausage, he fell out
On a red hot cinder.
Brightly shone his bum that night
Though the frost was cruel,
When an old man came in sight
And said, 'You daft old fool!'

While shepherds washed their socks by night
While watching ITV
The angel of the Lord came down
And switched to BBC!

We three kings of Orient are
Trying to smoke a rubber cigar
It was loaded
It exploded
Now we are seeing stars!

Oh star of wonder, star of night
Sit on a pack of dynamite
Light the fuse and off we go
On our way to Mexico!

Good King Wenceslas looked out
On a cabbage garden.
He bumped into a Brussels sprout
And said, 'I beg your pardon!'

Carols that never became popular
Bad King Wenceslas
The Second Noel
A Whale in a Manger
I Saw Three Car Ferries Come Sailing In
O Little Town of Birmingham
Deck the Loo Seat with Boughs of Holly
It Came Upon a Midnight Cloudy
Noisy Night
See, Amid the Winter's Slush
Jangle Bells
While Shepherds Watched their TVs by Night

Also available for Amazon Kindle from Montpelier Publishing:

Non-Corny Knock Knock Jokes: 150 super funny jokes for kids

A Little Book of Limericks: funny rhymes for all the family

A Little Book of Ripping Riddles and Confounding Conundrums

More Ripping Riddles and Confounding Conundrums

Riddles in Rhyme

A Little Book of Parlour Puzzles

The Bumper Book of Riddles, Puzzles and Rhymes

The Book of Church Jokes: a collection of (mostly) clean Christian chuckles

After Dinner Laughs: jokes and funny stories for speech makers

After Dinner Laughs 2: more jokes and funny stories for speech makers

Scottish Jokes: a Wee Book of Clean Caledonian Chuckles (also in paperback)

Wedding Jokes: Hilarious Gags for your Best Man's Speech

Printed in Great Britain
by Amazon.co.uk, Ltd.,
Marston Gate.